VOLVO PENTA MD 11C, C, MD 17C, D

Workshop Manual

VOLVO PENTA MD 11C, C, MD 17C, D

Workshop Manual

ISBN/EAN: 9783954275038
Erscheinungsjahr: 2012
Erscheinungsort: Bremen, Deutschland

© maritimepress in Europäischer Hochschulverlag GmbH & Co. KG, Fahrenheitstr. 1, 28359 Bremen. Alle Rechte beim Verlag und bei den jeweiligen Lizenzgebern.

www.maritimepress.de | office@maritimepress.de

Bei diesem Titel handelt es sich um den Nachdruck eines historischen, lange vergriffenen Buches. Da elektronische Druckvorlagen für diese Titel nicht existieren, musste auf alte Vorlagen zurückgegriffen werden. Hieraus zwangsläufig resultierende Qualitätsverluste bitten wir zu entschuldigen.

VOLVO PENTA MD 11C, C, MD 17C, D

Workshop Manual

Contents

Safety precautions 2
General Information 5
Repair instructions 6
Component guide 8

DISMANTLING
Cylinder head 10
Cylinder liner 11
Pistons, con-rods 11
Timing gear 12
Flywheel 13
Crankshaft 14
Camshaft 14

OVERHAULING
Dismantling cylinder head 15
Cleaning, inspection 15
Valve guides 15
Valve seats 16
Valves 16
Valve springs 16
Rocker mechanism 16
Valve tappets 16
Injector sleeve 17
Injector 17
Assembling cylinder head 18
Cleaning, checking crankcase 18
Replacing main bearings 18
Centrifugal governor 19
Pistons, liners 19
Connecting rods 20
Crankshaft 20
Camshaft 20
Oil pump 20
Feed pump 21
Thermostat 21
Sea water pump 21
Hand start 23

ASSEMBLING
Crankshaft 24
Flywheel 25
Timing gear 25
Cylinders, cylinder liners 27
Pistons and liners 28
Cylinder head 29
Adjusting valve clearance 30
Injection pump 31
Checking control rod travel 32
Venting the fuel system 33
Checking injections angle 34
Adjusting engine speed 34

Electrical system 35
Wiring diagram 35
Fault finding chart 36
Special tools 37
Technical data 39
Cooling system, diagrammatic sketch 43

Safety Precautions

Introduction

This Workshop Manual contains technical data, descriptions and repair instructions for Volvo Penta products or product versions contained in the contents list. Ensure that the correct workshop literature is being used.

Read the safety information and the Workshop Manual "General Information" and "Repair Instructions" carefully before starting work.

Important

In this book and on the engine you will find the following special warning symbols.

 WARNING! If these instructions are not followed there is a danger of personal injury, extensive damage to the product or serious mechanical malfunction.

 IMPORTANT! Used to draw your attention to something that can cause damage, product malfunction or damage to property.

NOTE! Used to draw your attention to important information that will facilitate work or operations.

Below is a summary of the risks and safety precautions you should always observe or carry out when operating or servicing the engine.

 Immobilize the engine by turning off the power supply to the engine at the main switch (switches) and lock it (them) in the OFF position before starting work. Set up a warning notice at the engine control point or helm.

 Generally, all servicing should be carried out with the engine switched off. Some work (carrying out certain adjustments for example) requires the engine to be running. Approaching a running engine is dangerous. Loose clothing or long hair can fasten in rotating parts and cause serious personal injury.
If working in proximity to a running engine, careless movements or a dropped tool can result in personal injury. Avoid burns. Take precautions to avoid hot surfaces (exhausts, turbochargers, charge air pipes and starter elements etc.) and liquids in supply lines and hoses when the engine is running or has been turned off immediately prior to starting work on it. Reinstall all protective parts removed during service operations before starting the engine.

 Check that the warning or information decals on the product are always clearly visible. Replace decals that have been damaged or painted over.

 Never use start spray or similar to start the engine. The starter element may cause an explosion in the inlet manifold. Danger of personal injury.

 Avoid opening the filler cap for engine coolant system (freshwater cooled engines) when the engine is still hot. Steam or hot coolant can spray out. Open the coolant filler cap carefully and slowly to release pressure before removing the cap completely. Take great care if a cock, plug or engine coolant line must be removed from a hot engine. It is difficult to anticipate in which direction steam or hot coolant can spray out.

 Hot oil can cause burns. Avoid skin contact with hot oil. Ensure that the lubrication system is not under pressure before commencing work on it. Never start or operate the engine with the oil filler cap removed, otherwise oil could be ejected.

 Stop the engine and close the sea cock before carrying out operations on the engine cooling system.

 Only start the engine in a well-ventilated area. If operating the engine in an enclosed space, ensure that exhaust gases and crankcase ventilation emissions are ventilated out of the working area.

 Always use protective goggles where there is a danger of pieces of metal, sparks from grinding, acid or other chemicals being thrown into your eyes. Your eyes are very sensitive, injury can lead to loss of sight!

Avoid skin contact with oil. Long-term or repeated contact with oil can remove the natural oils from your skin. The result can be irritation, dry skin, eczema and other skin problems. Used oil is more dangerous to health than new oil. Use protective gloves and avoid using oil-soaked clothes and rags. Wash regularly, especially before meals. Use the correct barrier cream to prevent dry skin and to make cleaning your skin easier.

 Most chemicals used in products (engine and transmission oils, glycol, petrol and diesel oil) and workshop chemicals (solvents and paints) are hazardous to health Read the instructions on the product packaging carefully! Always follow safety instructions (using breathing apparatus, protective goggles and gloves for example). Ensure that other personnel are not unwittingly exposed to hazardous substances (by breathing them in for example). Ensure that ventilation is good. Handle used and excess chemicals according to instructions.

 All fuels and many chemicals are inflammable. Ensure that a naked flame or sparks cannot ignite fuel or chemicals. Combined with air in certain ratios, petrol, some solvents and hydrogen from batteries are easily inflammable and explosive. Smoking is prohibited! Ensure that ventilation is good and that the necessary safety precautions have been taken before carrying out welding or grinding work. Always have a fire extinguisher to hand in the workplace.

 Store oil and fuel-soaked rags and fuel and oil filters safely. In certain conditions oil-soaked rags can spontaneously ignite. Used fuel and oil filters are environmentally dangerous waste and must be deposited at an approved site for destruction together with used lubricating oil, contaminated fuel, paint remnants, solvent, degreasing agents and waste from washing parts.

 Never allow a naked flame or electric sparks near the batteries. Never smoke in proximity to the batteries. The batteries give off hydrogen gas during charging which when mixed with air can form an explosive gas - oxyhydrogen. This gas is easily ignited and highly volatile. Incorrect connection of the battery can cause a spark which is sufficient to cause an explosion with resulting damage. Do not disturb battery connections when starting the engine (spark risk) and do not lean over batteries.

 Never mix up the positive and negative battery terminals when installing. Incorrect installation can result in serious damage to electrical equipment. Refer to wiring diagrams.

 Always use protective goggles when charging and handling batteries. The battery electrolyte contains extremely corrosive sulfuric acid. If this comes into contact with the skin, wash immediately with soap and plenty of water. If battery acid comes into contact with the eyes, immediately flush with copious amounts of water and obtain medical assistance.

 Turn off the engine and turn off power at main switch(es) before carrying out work on the electrical system.

 Use the lifting eyes mounted on the engine/reverse gear when lifting the drive unit.
Always check that lifting equipment is in good condition and has sufficient load capacity to lift the engine (engine weight including reverse gear and any extra equipment installed).

To ensure safe handling and to avoid damaging engine components on top of the engine, use a lifting beam to raise the engine. All chains and cables should run parallel to each other and as perpendicular as possible in relation to the top of the engine.

If extra equipment is installed on the engine altering its center of gravity, a special lifting device is required to achieve the correct balance for safe handling.

Never carry out work on an engine suspended on a hoist.

Never remove heavy components alone, even where secure lifting equipment such as secured blocks are being used. Even where lifting equipment is being used it is best to carry out the work with two people; one to operate the lifting equipment and the other to ensure that components are not trapped and damaged when being lifted. When working on-board ensure that there is sufficient space to remove components without danger of injury or damage.

 Components in the electrical system, ignition system (gasoline engines) and fuel system on Volvo Penta products are designed and constructed to minimize the risk of fire and explosion. The engine must not be run in areas where there are explosive materials.

 Always use fuels recommended by Volvo Penta. Refer to the Instruction Book. The use of lower quality fuels can damage the engine. On a diesel engine poor quality fuel can cause the control rod to seize and the engine to overrev with the resulting risk of damage to the engine and personal injury. Poor fuel quality can also lead to higher maintenance costs.

General information

About the workshop manual

This workshop manual contains technical specification, descriptions and instructions for repairing the standard versions of the following engines MD11C, D, MD17C, D. The workshop manual displays the operations carried out on any of the engines above. As a result the illustrations and pictures in the manual that show certain parts on the engines, do not in some cases apply to all the engines listed above. However the repair and service operations described are the same in all essential details. Where they are not the same this is stated in the manual and where the difference is considerable the operations are described separately. Engine designations and numbers are given on the number plate (See page 9). The engine designation and number should be given in all correspondence about the engine.

This Workshop Manual has been developed primarily for Volvo Penta service workshops and qualified personnel. Persons using this book are assumed to have a grounding in marine drive systems and be able to carry out related mechanical and electrical work.

Volvo Penta is continuously developing their products. We therefore reserve the right to make changes. All the information contained in this book is based on product data available at the time of going to print. Any essential changes or modifications introduced into production or updated or revised service methods introduced after the date of publication will be provided in the form of Service Bulletins.

Replacement parts

Replacement parts for electrical and fuel systems are subject to statutory requirements (US Coast Guard Safety Regulations for example). Volvo Penta Genuine parts meet these requirements. Any type of damage which results from the use of non-original Volvo Penta replacement parts for the product will not be covered under any warranty provided by Volvo Penta.

Repair instructions

The working methods described in the Service Manual apply to work carried out in a workshop. The engine has been removed from the boat and is installed in an engine fixture. Unless otherwise stated reconditioning work which can be carried out with the engine in place follows the same working method.

Warning symbols occurring in the Workshop Manual (for their meaning see *Safety information*)

 **WARNING!**

 **IMPORTANT!**

NOTE!

are not in any way comprehensive since it is impossible to predict every circumstance under which service work or repairs may be carried out. For this reason we can only highlight the risks that can arise when work is carried out incorrectly in a well-equipped workshop using working methods and tools developed by us.

All procedures for which there are Volvo Penta special tools in this Workshop Manual are carried out using these. Special tools are developed to rationalize working methods and make procedures as safe as possible. It is therefore the responsibility of any person using tools or working methods other than the ones recommended by us to ensure that there is no danger of injury, damage or malfunction resulting from these.

In some cases there may be special safety precautions and instructions for the use of tools and chemicals contained in this Workshop Manual. These special instructions should always be followed if there are no separate instructions in the Workshop Manual.

Certain elementary precautions and common sense can prevent most risks arising. A clean workplace and engine eliminates much of the danger of injury and malfunction.

It is of the greatest importance that no dirt or foreign particles get into the fuel system, lubrication system, intake system, turbocharger, bearings and seals when they are being worked on. The result can be malfunction or a shorter operational life.

Our joint responsibility

Each engine consists of many connected systems and components. If a component deviates from its technical specification the environmental impact of an otherwise good engine may be increased significantly. It is therefore vital that wear tolerances are maintained, that systems that can be adjusted are adjusted properly and that Volvo Penta Genuine Parts as used. The engine Maintenance Schedule must be followed.

Some systems, such as the components in the fuel system, require special expertise and special testing equipment for service and maintenance. Some components are sealed at the factory for environmental reasons. No work should be carried out on sealed components except by authorized personnel.

Bear in mind that most chemicals used on boats are harmful to the environment if used incorrectly. Volvo Penta recommends the use of biodegradable degreasing agents for cleaning engine components, unless otherwise stated in a workshop manual. Take special care when working on-board, that oil and waste is taken for destruction and is not accidentally pumped into the environment with bilge water.

Tightening torques

Tightening torques for vital joints that must be tightened with a torque wrench are listed in workshop manual "Technical Data": "Tightening Torques" and are contained in work descriptions in this Manual. All torques apply for cleaned threads, screw heads and mating surfaces. Torques apply for lightly oiled or dry threads. If lubricants, locking fluid or sealing compound are required for a screwed joint this information will be contained in the work description and in "Tightening Torques" Where no tightening torque is stated for a joint use the general tightening torques according to the tables below. The tightening torques stated are a guide and the joint does not have to be tightened using a torque wrench.

Dimension	Tightening Torques	
	Nm	lbt.ft
M5	6	4.4
M6	10	7.4
M8	25	18.4
M10	50	36.9
M12	80	59.0
M14	140	103.3

Tightening torques-protractor (angle) tightening

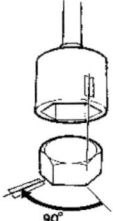

Tightening using both a torque setting and a protractor angle requires that first the recommended torque is applied using a torque wrench and then the recommended angle is added according to the protractor scale. Example: a 90° protractor tightening means that the joint is tightened a further 1/4 turn in one operation after the stated tightening torque has been applied.

Locknuts

Do not re-use lock nuts that have been removed during dismantling as they have reduced service life when re-used - use new nuts when assembling or re-installing. For lock nuts with a plastic insert such as Nylock® the tightening torque stated in the table is reduced if the Nylock® nut has the same head height as a standard hexagonal nut without plastic insert. Reduce the tightening torque by 25% for bolt size 8 mm or larger. Where Nylock® nuts are higher, or of the same height as a standard hexagonal nut, the tightening torques given in the table apply.

Tolerance classes

Screws and nuts are divided into different strength classes, the class is indicated by the number on the bolt head. A high number indicates stronger material, for example a bolt marked 10-9 indicates a higher tolerance than one marked 8-8. It is therefore important that bolts removed during the disassembly of a bolted joint must be reinstalled in their original position when assembling the joint. If a bolt must be replaced check in the replacement parts catalogue to make sure the correct bolt is used.

Sealants

A number of sealants and locking liquids are used on the engines. The agents have varying properties and are used for different types of jointing strengths, operating temperature ranges, resistance to oil and other chemicals and for the different materials and gap sizes in the engines.

To ensure service work is correctly carried out it is important that the correct sealant and locking fluid type is used on the joint where the agents are required.

In this Volvo Penta Service Manual the user will find that each section where these agents are applied in production states which type was used on the engine.

During service operations use the same agent or an alternative from a different manufacturer.

Make sure that mating surfaces are dry and free from oil, grease, paint and anti-corrosion agent before applying sealant or locking fluid. Always follow the manufacturer's instructions for use regarding; temperature range, curing time and any other instructions for the product.

Two different basic types of agent are used on the engine and these are:

RTV agent (Room temperature vulcanizing). Use for gaskets, sealing gasket joints or coating gaskets. RTV agent is clearly visible when a component has been dismantled; old RTV must be removed before the joint is resealed. Old sealant can be removed using methylated spirits in all cases.

Anaerobic agents. These agents cure in an absence of air. They are used when two solid parts, for example cast components, are installed face-to-face without a gasket. They are also commonly used to secure plugs, threads in stud bolts, cocks, oil pressure switches and so on. The cured material is glass-like and it is therefore colored to make it visible. Cured anaerobic agents are extremely resistant to solvents and the old agent cannot be removed. When reinstalling the part is carefully degreased and then new sealant is applied.

Component guide

MD11C and D

1. Stop device
2. Air bleed screw, injection pump
3. Injector
4. Delivery pipe nut
5. Temperature sender
6. Lock-screw, crankshaft centre bearing
7. Drain cocks, cooling water
8. Inspection cover
9. Oil drain plug, engine
10. Oil dipstick, reverse gear
11. Oil filler, reverse gear
12. Oil drain plug, reverse gear
13. Water drain plug, reverse gear (MD11D, connection hose)
14. Decompression handle (certain models)
15. Air filter
16. Oil filler, engine
17. Pressure equalizing valve (certain models)
18. Air bleed screw
19. Fine filter
20. Feed pump
21. Engine speed sender
22. Oil filter
23. Oil pressure sender
24. Oil strainer and oil dipstick (MD11C)
25. Oil pump
26. Oil dipstick, MD11D

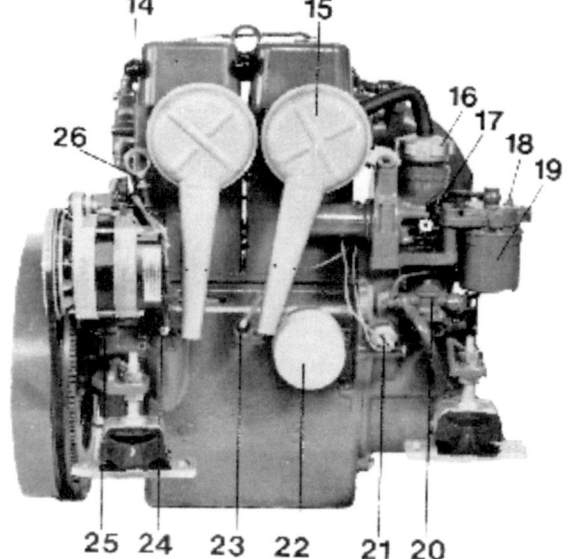

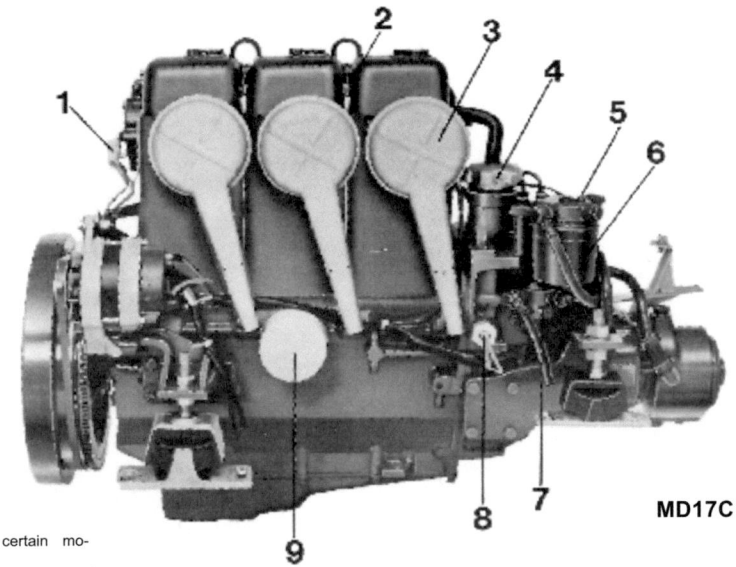

MD17C and D

1. Fuse box
2. Decompression handle, certain models
3. Air filter
4. Oil filler
5. Air bleed screw
6. Fine filter
7. Feed pump
8. Engine speed sender
9. Oil filter
10. Stop device
11. Adjustment screw - high idle speed
12. Adjustment screw - low idle speed
13. Leak-off pipe
14. Lifting eye
15. Delivery pipe
16. Injector
17. Thermostat housing
18. Oil dipstick
19. Drain cocks, cooling water
20. Engine type and number plate
21. Cooling water pump

Dismantling

Drain off the engine cooling water, lubricating oil and any fuel in the fuel filter and fuel injection pump. Clean the outside of the engine.

2B. The picture shows later type of injector from and including engine no. 50989 (MD11) and 16622 (MD17).

1. A fixture for securing the engine in the engine stand 9992520 may be used to advantage. MD11: 884604. MD17: 884581.

3. Take off the coolant pipe between the sea water pump and the exhaust manifold. Remove the exhaust manifold (wrench width 13 mm).

CYLINDER HEAD

2A. Take off the air cleaner, the leak-off oil pipe and the delivery pipes. Fit protective caps.
The picture shows earlier type of injector up to and including engine no. 50988 (MD11) and 16621 (MD17).

4. Remove the valve covers. Undo the oil pipes on the rocker arm shafts and dismantle the rocker arm bearing brackets. Take out the push rods.

5. Remove the eyebolt (or eyebolts) and nuts holding the cylinder heads (wrench width 19 mm). Straighten out the oil pipes slightly and lift the cylinder heads off.

6A. Disconnect the cables from the engine speed sender, the oil pressure switch and the alternator. MD11: Remove the alternator bracket together with the alternator. The picture shows the earlier model MD11C up to and including engine no. 52480 and MD11D from production start. MD17: Remove the cover (earlier models) over the V-belt and remove the alternator.

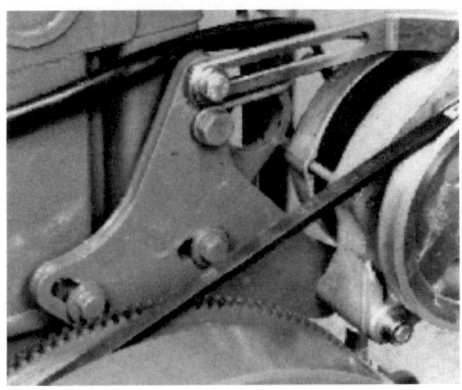

6B. MD11C: The picture shows the later models from and including engine no. 52481.

CYLINDERS, CYLINDER LINERS

7. Lift the cylinders out. Remove the cylinder liners by placing the cylinder with the bottom of the liner on a flat support and strike the top face of the cylinder with a rubber mallet.

PISTONS AND CONNECTING RODS

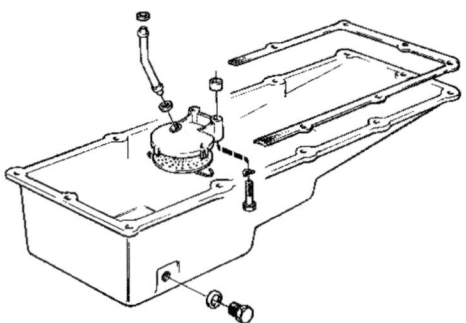

8. MD11: Remove the inspection covers on the crankcase (6 mm socket head). MD17: Remove the oil sump and strainer. NOTE! Remove the sealing rings in the ends of the oil pump suction pipe.

9. Remove the big-end bearing caps and take out the connecting rods (and pistons). Mark the connecting rods (if this has not already been done). Remove the valve tappets.

TIMING GEAR

10. Remove the crankcase breather/hand starter.

13A. **MD11C and MD17C.** Remove the carrier on the crankshaft (engines with RB-reverse gear have a carrier drive, use a distance piece to protect the shaft. Take care of the key.

11. Remove the injection pump, sea water pump, feed pump and the fuel filter.
    The D-engines have leak-off oil return pipes connected to the inlet union (see also page 27).

13B. **MD11D and MD17D.** Remove the carrier on the crankshaft. Use puller 884078 (for the flywheel), use a distance piece to protect the shaft. Take care of the key. Earlier types of puller 884078 can be modified by drilling three Ø 8.5 mm holes (use the spline flange as a template).

12. Take off the timing gear cover.

14. Pull off the crankshaft gear with the aid of tool 884078. Remove the key, the spacing washer and the thrust washer.

15. Unscrew the left handed carrier screw/nut on the camshaft. Pull out the cam disc and the gearwheel together. (On MD11, the crankshaft can be dismantled without taking off the camshaft gearwheel).

18. Remove the starter motor and its bracket.

16. MD11, certain models: Remove the belt pulley that is mounted on the flywheel. MD17: Remove the bearing shield.

19. Remove the oil pump.

FLYWHEEL

17. Bend out the lock washer and unscrew the central nut. Pull off the flywheel using the puller 884078. Take care of the key. NOTE! The nut is pulled using 500 Nm (50 kpm = 369 lbf.ft.)

20. MD11: Remove the front engine brackets. Remove the bearing shield.

CRANKSHAFT

21. Remove the locating screw for the crankshaft centre bearing (two in the case of MD17). Pull the crankshaft out.

23B. MD11C. Tool 884714.

23C. MD11D. Hexagon, 30 mm.

CAMSHAFT

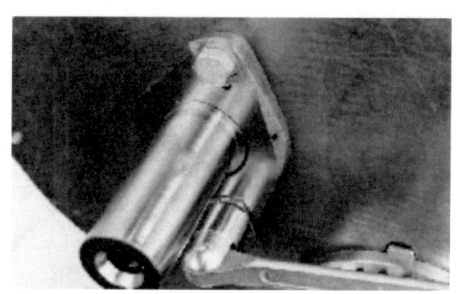

22. Remove the thrust washer and lift the camshaft out. MD17: Check that the oil hole is correctly located when re-assembling.

24. Loosen the lock screw and remove the centrifugal governor.

23A. Remove the oil filter, the oil pressure switch and the oil pipes for the rocker arm mechanism. MD11: Remove the oil strainer. MD11C: Use tool 884714 (see 23B). MD11D: 30 mm hexagon (see 23C).

25. Unscrew the centre bearing (MD17, two bearings). NOTE! Mark them so that they can be re-fitted in the same positions.

Overhauling

Cylinder head
DISMANTLING

26. Remove the injectors and fit protective caps on the tips of the nozzles.

27. Remove the wear caps from the valve stems. Remove the valve springs with the aid of a valve spring compressor. Place the valves in order in a valve stand. Take off the sealing rings that are fitted on the valve guides.

CLEANING, INSPECTION

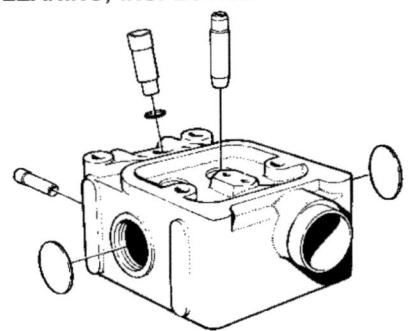

28. Clean all parts. Pay particular attention to coolant passages. In case of doubt, check for leakage by pressure testing. Water pressure 0.3 MPa (3 kg/cm^2 = 43 p.s.i.).

VALVE GUIDES

29. Check the valve guides for wear by inserting a new valve. Measure the clearance with the aid of a dial gauge. Replace the guides if necessary.
Wear limits:
Inlet valve,
max. clearance .... 0.15 mm (0.00591")
Exhaust valve,
max. clearance .... 0.17 mm (0.00669")

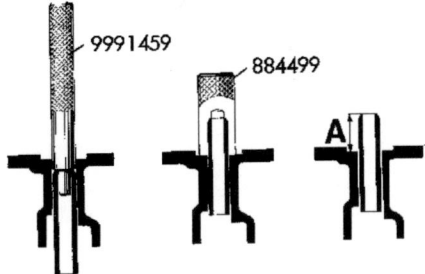

A = 18 mm (0.709")

30. Press out the valve guides using drift 9991459. Oil the new guides externally and press them into position with tool 884499. The tool should be pressed right down against the cylinder head. Ream the guides if necessary with broach 9994128.

VALVE SEATS AND VALVES

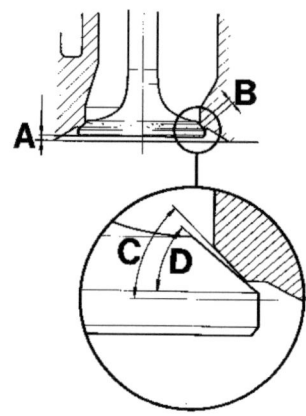

A = max 2.5 mm (0.10")   C = 45°
B = 1±0.1 mm (0.040±0.004")   D = 44,5°

31. Mill or ream the valve seats, the angle (C) should be 45°. Check the valve guides and replace them if necessary before machining the seats, see point 29. The width (B) of the sealing surface should be 1±0.1 mm (0.040"±0.004"). Grind the valves in the valve grinding machine. The angle (D) should be 44.5°. If the thickness of the edge of the disc after grinding is less than 1.5 mm (0.059"), the valve should be rejected. Discard also valves with bent stems or if the dimension (A) exceeds 2.5 mm (0.10"). If necessary grind the surface on which the rocker arm bears. Grind the valves in using grinding compound and check the surface contact using marking blue.

ROCKER ARM MECHANISM

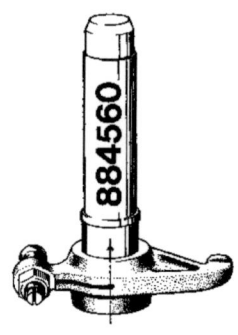

33. Dismantle the rocker arm mechanism and clean the parts. Check the shaft and the bushes for wear. If the bushes need to be replaced, the tool 884560 is used for pressing out and in. (Ensure that the oil hole in the bush coincides with that in the rocker arm). After having been pressed in, the bushes should be reamed to give an accurate running fit. Check whether the rocker arm surface which bears on the valve is worn. Minor adjustments can be made with the valve grinding machine. Oil the shaft and fit the parts.
NOTE! Fit the wear caps on the valve stems.

VALVE SPRINGS

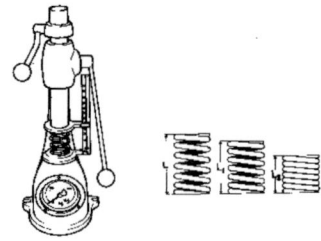

32. Check the valve spring lengths both loaded and unloaded.
L   Length unloaded .... 50 mm (1.969")
L_1 Length when loaded with
       300±20 N (30±2 kp = 66.6±4.41 lbf) .... 39 mm (1.535")
L_2 Length when loaded with
       560±30 N (56±3 kp = 123.5±6.6 lbf) .... 32 mm (1.26")

VALVE TAPPETS

34. Check the valve tappets for wear. The cylindrical surface should not be scored or porous. The surface bearing on the camshaft should not be rough or worn unevenly. Replace the tappets if necessary.

INJECTOR SLEEVE

Drain the engine cooling water, if this has not already been done.

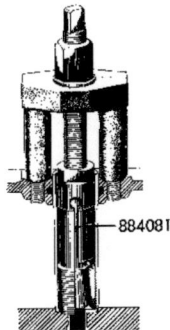

35. Remove the sleeve using the tool 884081. Push the expanding screw down into the sleeve and screw anti-clockwise so that the screw expands and grips the sleeve. Tighten until the threads bite into the copper material. Fit the yoke onto the stud bolts which hold the injector. Screw on the nut and rotate until the sleeve is removed.

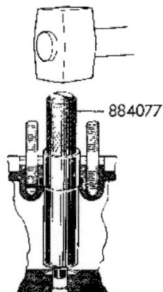

36. Remove the O-ring and carefully clean the hole in which the sleeve is to fit. Grease and fit the new O-ring. Oil the new sleeve and fit it using tool 884077. Knock the sleeve in until it bottoms.

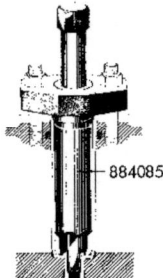

37. Oil-in the flaring tool 884085 and push it into the sleeve (make sure that the pin is screwed back correctly). Place nuts or washers on the stud bolts so that the yoke can be clamped tightly with the nuts. Screw the tool down as far as the shoulder in the sleeve permits, thus flaring the sleeve. Remove the tool.

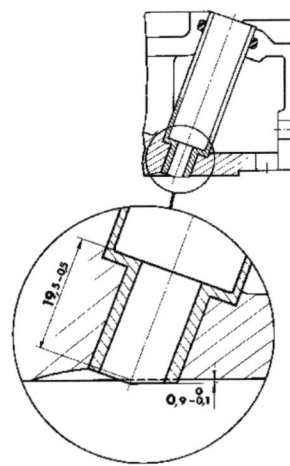

38. Adjust the length of the sleeve outside the plane of the cylinder head (dimension 0.9 mm, 0.035"). Also check that the sleeve is correctly fitted (dimension 19.5 mm, 0.768").

INJECTORS

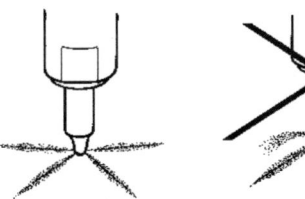

39. Check the spray pattern at the correct opening pressure. Up to and including engine no. 50988 (MD11), 16621 (MD17):

$17.0 ^{+\ 0.8}_{-\ 0}$ MPa ($170 ^{+\ 0.8}_{-\ 0}$ kp/cm² = $2418 ^{+\ 114}_{-\ 0}$ p.s.i.)

From and including engine no. 50989 (MD11), 16622 (MD17):

$24.5 ^{+\ 0.8}_{-\ 0}$ MPa ($245 ^{+\ 0.8}_{-\ 0}$ kp/cm² = $3485 ^{+\ 114}_{-\ 0}$ p.s.i.)

Also check that the fuel jets cease simultaneously at all four holes and that there is no "dribble" afterwards.

Crankcase

CLEANING AND INSPECTION

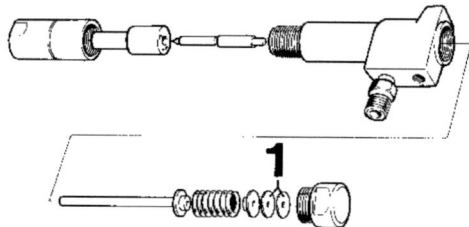

Up to and including engine no. 50988 (MD11), 16621 (MD17).

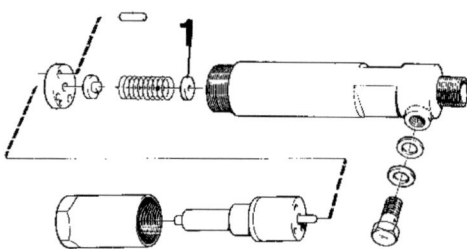

From and including engine no. 50989 (MD11), 16622 (MD17).

40. The opening pressure is adjusted by means of screwing the injector apart and replacing the adjusted washer (1) with a washer of suitable thickness.

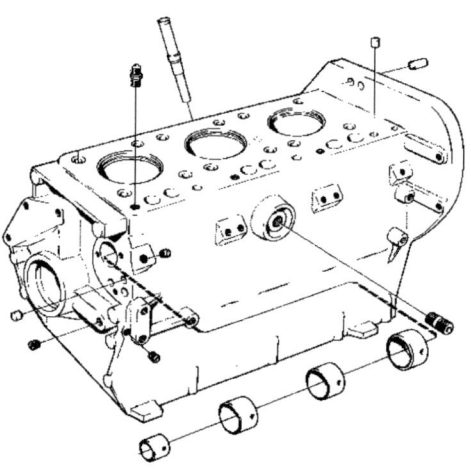

42. Remove all core plugs and clean the crankcase thoroughly. Check that all channels are free from deposits and that there are no cracks in the crankcase. Refit the plugs using a sealing compound.

ASSEMBLING THE CYLINDER HEAD

REPLACEMENT OF MAIN BEARINGS

41A. Clean the cylinder head. Oil the new sealing rings for the inlet valves. Place the pin of tool No. 884497 in the valve guide. Push the seal ring over the pin and knock the ring down carefully using the sleeve until the pin bottoms in the sleeve.

B. Oil the valve stems and smear a little grease in the inlet valve collet grooves. Place the valves in their respective guides, screw the inlet valves in carefully so as to avoid damaging the sealing rings. Fit the valve springs with the aid of a valve spring compressor.

43. Press the main bearings out using tool 884489 or a hydraulic press. NOTE! Check the positions of the locking tongues so that the bearing is removed in the right direction. Clean the oil channels before fitting new bearings.

PISTONS, LINERS

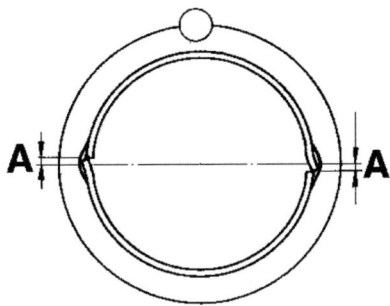

A = 1.5 mm (0.06")

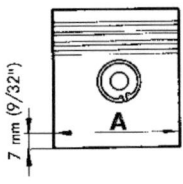 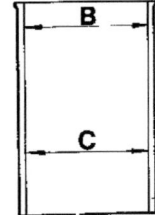

44A. Fit the two halves of the new bearing together with an elastic cord and turn them so that the locking tongues after pressing in fit into the appropriate recess. NOTE! The halves should be slightly staggered, see the diagram.

44B. Press the bearings in with tool 884489 or using a hydraulic press.

CENTRIFUGAL GOVERNOR

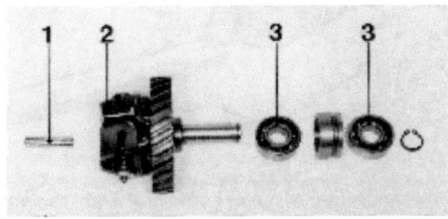

45. Clean the governor. Check that the weights (2) do not bind on the shaft or that there is excessive clearance between the shaft and the governor weights. Check that the pin (1) slides freely in the shaft. Finally, inspect both the ball bearings (3).
Replace the ball bearings if they bind. Check that all moving parts are oiled and move freely before assembling in reverse order.

46. Check the pistons and liners for damage and wear.
A. Measure the cylinder liners diameter at a number of points round the circumference and at several different heights between the top and bottom dead centre positions. (B and C). Replace the pistons and the liners if the wear amounts to 0.25 mm (0.01") or more.
B. Measure the piston diameter (A) at right angles to the gudgeon pin hole and 7 mm from the bottom edge. Calculate the maximum and minimum piston clearance (the maximum and minimum liner diameter minus the piston diameter).
Piston clearance (new): 0.09-0.13 mm (0.0035"-0.005").

47. Measure the piston ring gap with the new rings. If the cylinder liner is not new the measurement should be made below the bottom dead centre position. For dimension, see "Technical Data".

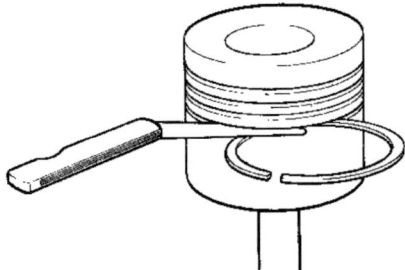

48. Measure the piston ring clearances in the piston ring grooves. For dimensions, see "Technical Data".

CONNECTING RODS

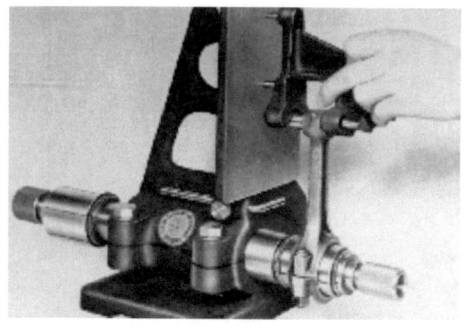

49. Check the connecting rods for straightness and twist.

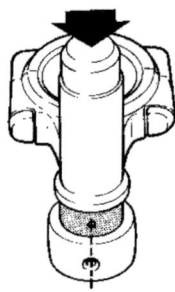

50. Check the connecting rod bushings, using the gudgeon pins as gauges. There should be no noticeable play. If it is necessary to replace the bushings a suitable drift should be used for pressing in and out. Ensure that the oil hole in bushings coincides with that in the connecting rod.

   Ream the new bushings. The correct fit is achieved when an oiled gudgeon pin slides slowly through the bushing under its own weight.

CRANKSHAFT

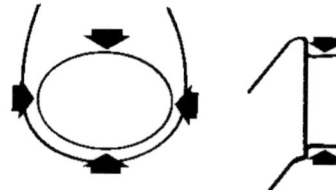

51. Measure the big end journals and the main bearing journals. The out-of-round should not exceed 0.06 mm (0.0024") and the taper should not exceed 0.05 mm (0.002"). If these values are exceeded, the crankshaft should be ground to a suitable undersize (see "Technical Data").

CAMSHAFT

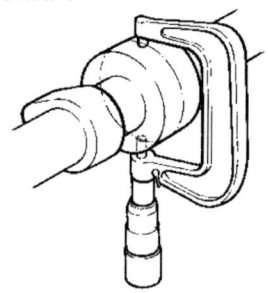

52. Check the camshaft for wear on the cams and bearing journals. Also check the wear on the bearings. The bearings are pressed into their recesses and must be line milled after pressing in. The maximum allowable wear on journals or bearings is 0.05 mm (0.002").

OIL PUMP

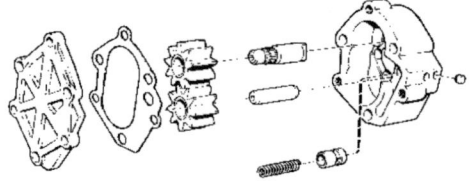

53. Remove the cover, retaining the old gasket. Remove the gearwheels, the spring and the piston. Clean all parts. Check the reducing valve spring, see "Technical Data". Replace any worn or damaged parts.

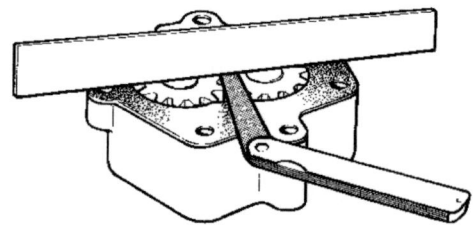

54A. Check the axial play of the gearwheels. NOTE! The old gasket should be included in the measurement. If necessary, the number of gaskets may be increased or reduced so as to obtain a clearance of 0.03-0.15 mm (0.001"-0.006"). The thickness of a new gasket is 0.10 mm (0.004"). Also inspect the cover, repair or replace as necessary if badly worn. Coat the gasket(s) with sealant and refit the parts. Pour a little oil into the pump before mounting onto the engine.

B. Check the gear backlash, which should be 0.15-0.35 mm (0.006-0.014"), using a feeler gauge. Worn gears must be replaced.

FEED PUMP

55. Undo the central screw in the cover, lift out the strainer and clean it. Take out the six screws holding the upper and lower parts of the pump together. Take out the lever spring (1), also remove the screw (2).

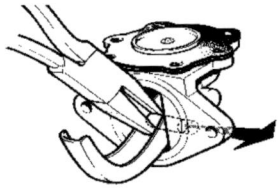

56. Remove the lever shaft using a pair of fine-nosed pliers. Pull out the lever and the diaphragm. Fit new parts from the repair kit and reassemble the pump.

THERMOSTAT

57. The thermostat is accessible after the thermostat housing on the front on the exhaust manifold has been taken off. Watch out for water pouring into the boat. Check the opening and closing temperatures with hot water. These should be as given in "Technical Data". If the thermostat is faulty it should be discarded. Use new sealing rings when refitting (MD17 has only one sealing ring). The picture shows the earlier type (bellows thermostat). Later engines are fitted with a wax thermostat.

SEA WATER PUMP

Replacing the impeller

58. Remove the cover. **Watch out for water pouring through the pump.** With the aid to two screwdrivers prise the shaft with the impeller out of the housing sufficiently for the screw which holds the impeller to be undone. NOTE! Lay some kind of protection under the screwdrivers so that the housing is not damaged.

59. Take the screw out and pull the impeller off the shaft. Clean the housing internally and check that the carrier (MD17) is free from defects and fit the new impeller. Fit the cover together with a new gasket.

60. **MD11: Engine no. 46159-46175 and from and including engine no. 46214.** Remove the cover. The impeller can be pulled out as shown in the picture or by using suitable pliers. NOTE! Protect the edge of the pump housing. The shaft follows with the impeller but is stopped by a pin behind the seals.

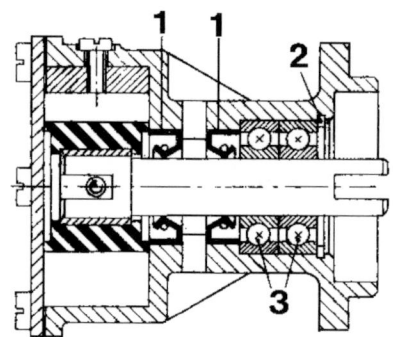

61. **MD17 from and including engine no. 17973 and MD17 - HD - HE from production start.**
The impeller is removed as shown in picture 60. The pump is fitted with two ball bearings (3). When disassembling, loosen the lock ring (2) and press out the shaft (the bearings following with the shaft). Press the bearings from the shaft using a suitable drift. When assembling, the bearings are pressed onto the shaft using drift 884742 until the shaft bottoms in the drift. The seals (1) are replaced according to point 63. Smear the shaft with grease and screw it carefully through the sealing rings so as not to damage them. Press in the shaft until the bearing bottoms and fit the lock ring (2).

Replacing the sealing rings

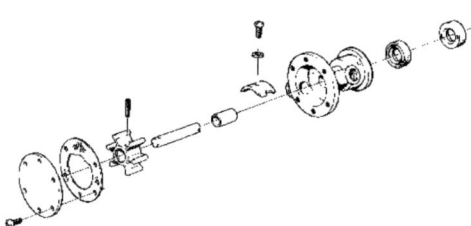

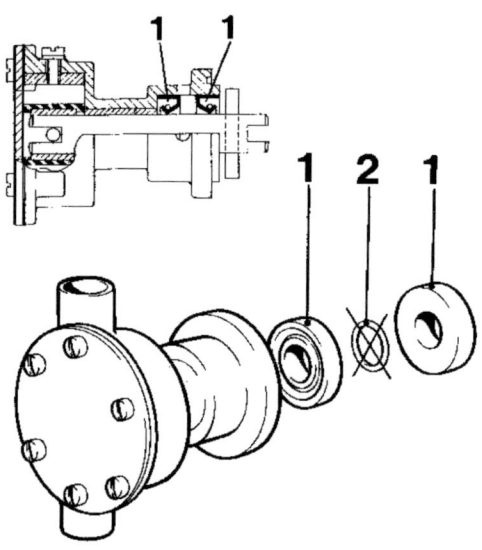

63. Remove the sealing rings (1) and the O-rings (2) (earlier engines) and clean the pump housing and shaft. Replace the impeller if necessary. Check that the shaft is free from burrs or scratches. Inspect the carrier (MD17). NOTE! A new O-ring (2) shall **not** be fitted.

    Fit new sealing rings. NOTE! Turn the sealing rings the right way round and ensure that they do not block the drainage hole in the pump housing. Smear the shaft with grease and fit it carefully into the housing, screwing it through the sealing rings to avoid damaging them.

    Locate the shaft in the housing so that the screw hole lies outside: Fit the impeller and the screw.

    Pump having open shaft. The shaft has a groove which is open at the front which is why the impeller is assembled with the screw fitted. Push the impeller in until bottoms.

    Fit a new gasket into the cover and secure it with the screws.

    Also check the carrier screw on the camshaft.

62. Remove the sea water pump. Watch out for water pouring into the boat. Take off the cover and press out the shaft and the impeller.

HAND STARTER, MD17

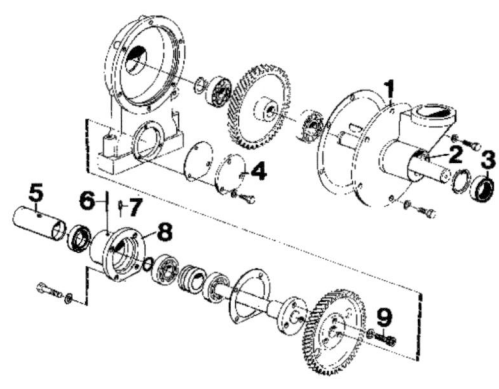

HAND STARTER, MD11

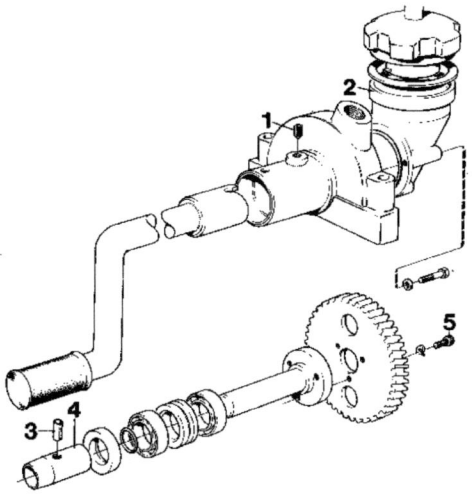

64. Remove the cover (1) together with the drive and shaft. Knock out the pin (2) and press the shaft out. Remove the sealing ring (3).
Remove the cover (4) and the screws (9), take off the gearwheel. Remove the bearing housing (8), knock out the pin (6) and pull out the sleeve (5). Take out the locking screw (7) and press out the shaft, the bearings, the spacer sleeve and the sealing rings.
Fit new sealing rings and replace any parts that are worn or damaged. Pack the bearings in with grease and refit the parts.

65. Remove the oil filler pipe (2). Undo the screws and take the gearwheel off. Knock out the locking pin (3) and take off the sleeve (4). Take out the locking screw (1) and press out the shaft, the bearings, the spacer sleeve and the sealing rings.
Fit the new sealing rings and replace any parts that are worn or damaged. Pack the bearings in with grease and refit the parts.

Assembling

Use new gaskets, sealing rings, sealing washers and lock washers. Grease or oil the sealing rings and oil moving parts before fitting.

CRANKSHAFT

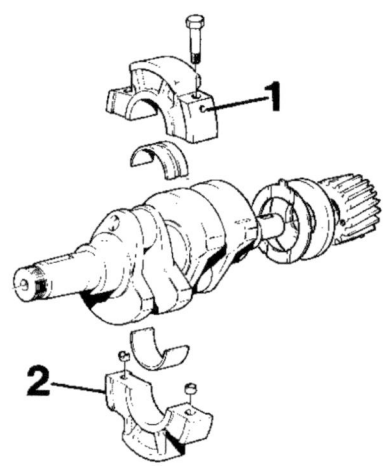

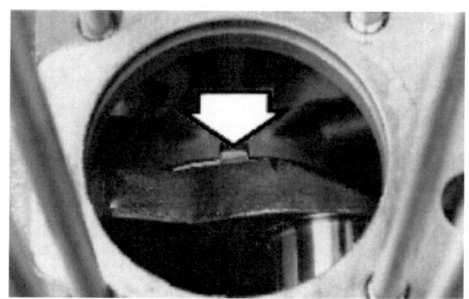

68. Fit the crankshaft in the crankcase. Ensure that the hole for the centre bearing locating screw lines up with the hole in the crankcase. MD11: Make sure that the lug on the thrust washer fits into the recess in the crankcase.

66. Fit the centre bearing (or bearings) on the crankshaft. NOTE! Turn the bearing the right way round so that the locating screw in the crankcase fits into the hole (2) in the centre bearing. "1" oil passage, "2" hole for locating screw.

69. Replace the O-ring on the centre bearing locating screw. Wind-on a little thread-sealing tape and apply Permatex to the outside. Screw the locating screw in so that it bottoms properly and then loosen it by half a turn.

67. MD11. Smear the two thrust washers with grease and fit one of them on the crankshaft turning the flat side towards the rear main bearing (timing gear side). The other washer is fitted in point 74.

70. MD11: Replace both O-rings on the bearing shield, see illustration. Replace the crankshaft sealing ring. Stick a small piece of tape over the keyway in the crankshaft and fit the bearing shield.

MD17: Stick a small piece of tape over the keyway in the crankshaft and fit a new sealing ring.

71. Fit the starter motor and the oil pump. NOTE! Put a little oil into the pump before fitting. MD11: Fit the front engine brackets.

74. Place the engine so that it is resting on the flywheel. Make sure that the inner thrust washer is correctly located. Place the outer thrust washer on the crankshaft with the flat surface towards the main bearing. Fit the distance washer with the flat surface toward the thrust washer.

FLYWHEEL

 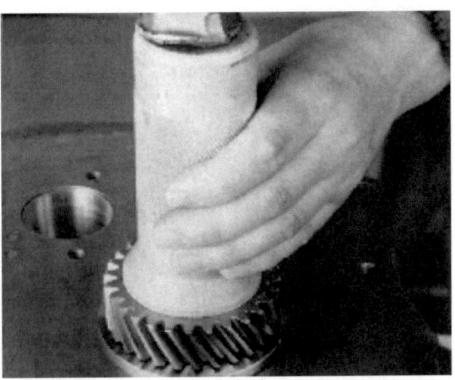

72. Fit the key and the flywheel (the taper must be perfectly clean). Tightening torque 500 Nm (50 kpm = 369 lbf.ft). Lock the nut by bending up the washer.

75. Fit the key for the crankshaft drive. Heat the gearwheel to about 100°C (212°F) and fit it onto the crankshaft. Check to make sure that the inner thrust washer does not move from its correct position.

TIMING GEAR

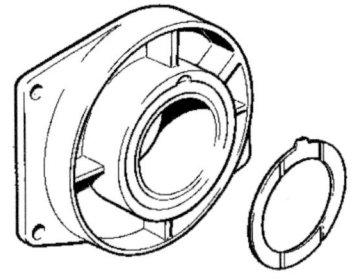 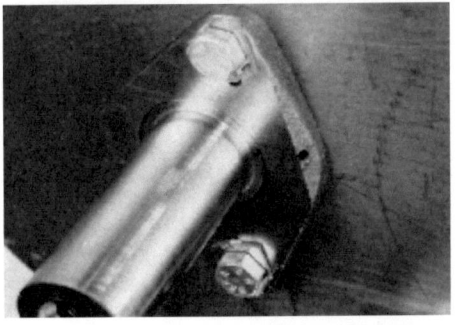

73. MD17: Smear both thrust washers with grease and place one of them on the inner side of the bearing shield, turning the flat side towards the main bearing. Ensure that the lug on the washer fits into the recess in the shield. Fit the bearing shield onto the engine and tighten the screws.

76. Fit the camshaft and ensure that the oil pump shaft fits into the slot in the camshaft. Lock the screws with the lock washers. MD17: Note the location of the oil passage.

25

77. Fit the camshaft drive key. Heat the gearwheel to about 100°C (212°F) and fit it so that the markings coincide. Fit the camshaft key.

78. Fit the cam disc and the left hand threaded screw/nut to the camshaft. Tightening torque: 70 Nm (7 kpm = 50 lbf.ft.) for MD11 and 320 Nm (32 kpm = 231 lbf.ft.) for MD17. Check the end play. This should be: 0.05-0.15 mm (0.002"-0.006").

79. Fit the key for the reverse gear carrier/carrier drive in crankshaft keyway on the reverse gear side. Heat the carrier/carrier drive to about 150°C (302°F) and fit it onto the crankshaft. Fit the large washer and the lock washer and tighten the screw with a torque wrench. Use a counterhold (in the flywheel).
Tightening torque:
MD11C and D .... 70 Nm (7 kpm = 50 lbf.ft.)
MD17C .... 120 Nm (12 kpm = 87 lbf.ft.)
MD17D .... 110 Nm (11 kpm = 80 lbf.ft.)
NOTE! At this torque the crankshaft drive is also completely tightened. Check the crankshaft axial play which should be 0.08-0.35 mm (0.003"-0.014"). Bend the lock washer against the head of the screw. C-engines, see 81A. D-engines, see 81 B.

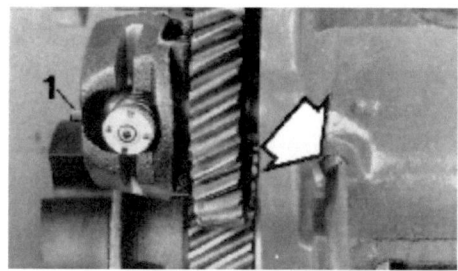

80. Fit the centrifugal governor. Tighten the socket-head screw on the side. NOTE! Make sure that the screw locates in the groove. Check that the pin (1) slides freely in the shaft. MD17: Fit the sea water pump carrier.

81A. MD11C and MD17C. Fit the timing gear cover.

81B. MD11D and MD17D. Fit the timing gear cover.

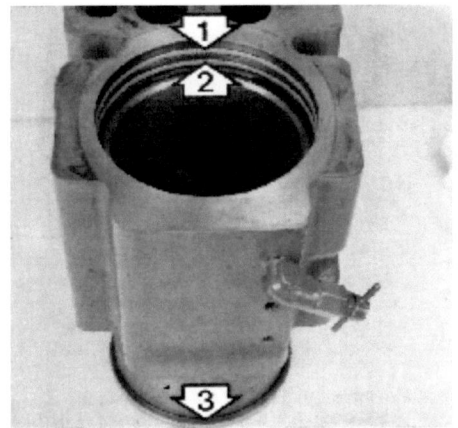

82. Fit the oil pipes for the rocker arm mechanism. Fit the oil pressure switch and a new oil filter. MD11: Fit the oil strainer. NOTE! Apply Permatex to the filter's sealing surface and threads and tighten the cover firmly (use a torque wrench), so that no air can get in and upset the lubrication. NOTE! Don't forget the gasket.
Tightening torque:
MD11C, 70 Nm (7 kpm = 50 lbf.ft.), tool 884714 "A".
MD11D, 120 Nm (12 kpm = 87 lbf.ft.), wrench width 30 mm "B".

84. Place the sealing rings into the cylinder grooves and under the liner collar. "1" yellow O-ring, "2" black O-ring and "3" black O-ring (narrow). Smear the rings with grease.

CYLINDERS AND CYLINDER LINERS

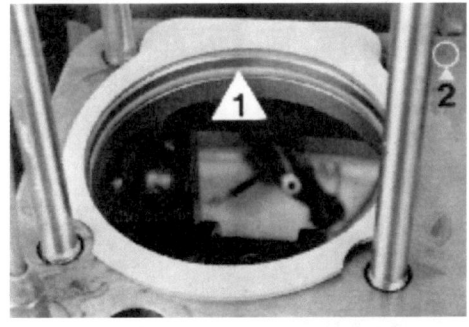

83. Grease and fit the sealing ring (yellow O-ring) for each respective cylinder liner in the groove in the crankcase (1). Place new shims on the crankcase face. **If the cylinder liners are not being replaced**, the equivalent shim thickness, which corresponds to the figure stamped on the crankcase surface for each respective cylinder (2) can be selected. The marking can be in the form of punch marks or figures which represent 1/10 mm (0.004"). **If new cylinder liners are fitted**, fit one 0.2 mm (0.008") and one 0.3 mm (0.012") shim for each cylinder. Later (when carrying out control measurements) one of the shims may be removed, if necessary, after having been clipped. Fit the valve tappets.

85. Place the liner with the collar against a support and put the cylinder onto the liner. Press down by hand until the collar rests against the counter bore in the cylinder. Make sure that the sealing rings are not forced out of position during this operation.

PISTONS AND LINERS

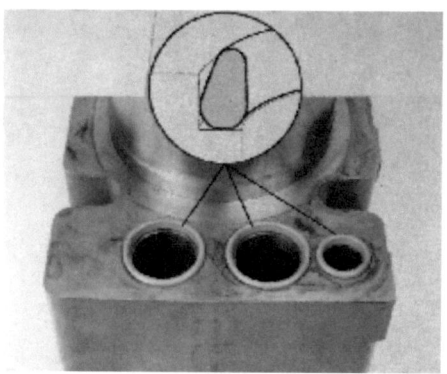

86. Fit the sealing rings for the push-rods and oil pipe channels. The rings should be turned so that the narrow edges seal against the crankcase. Smear a little grease on the rings.

88. Heat the pistons to about 100°C (212°F). Assemble the pistons and connecting rods as shown in the illustration.

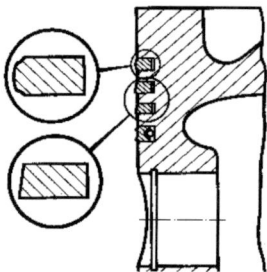

89. Fit the piston rings using piston ring pliers. It is immaterial which way up the upper ring and the oil scraper ring are fitted, but the other rings are marked "Top".
Turn the rings so that the gaps are staggered.

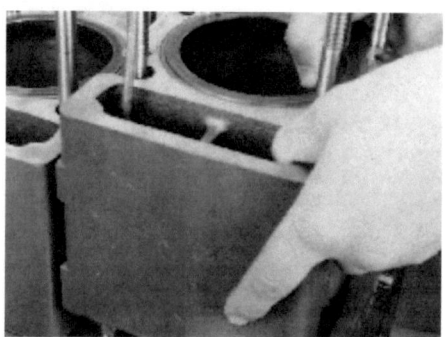

87. Place the cylinders on the crankcase.

90. Fit the pistons with the special tool 2823. This is the same as that used for the B20 and B30 engines. Fit piston No. 1 nearest to the timing gear. NOTE! The recess in the top of the piston must come immediately under the nozzle.

91. Fit the big-end bearing caps so that the engine markings agree. NOTE! New nuts and bolts should be used when assembling.
Tightening torque: 65 Nm (6.5 kpm = 47 lbf.ft.).

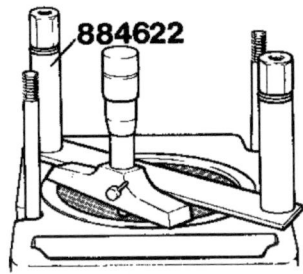

92. Press the cylinder liner down with tool 884622 and measure the distance "A" from the liner collar to the piston in the top dead centre position. See also Point 94.

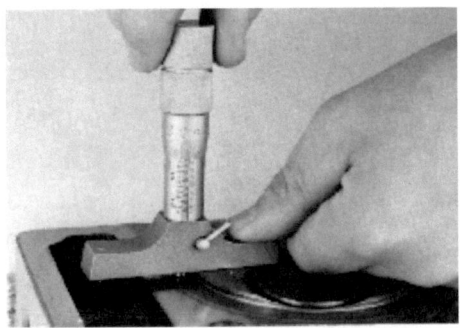

93. Measure the distance "B" from the downward projecting part of the cylinder head to the sealing plane. See also Point 94.

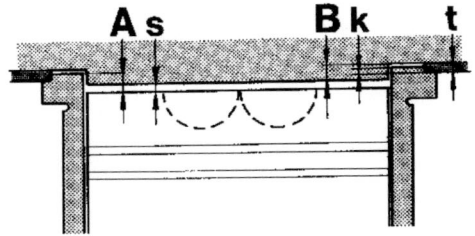

94. The value of 0.25 mm, (0.0098"), corresponding to t-k in the illustration is added to the dimension "A". Dimension "B" is subtracted from the result of this addition. The clearance "S" obtained should be 0.8-0.9 mm, (0.0315-0.0354"). If necessary, adjust the clearance with the shims under the cylinder.
Example: A = 4.40 mm, (0.173")
B = 3.53 mm, (0.139")
S = A+0.25-B, (A+0.01"-B)
S = 4.40+0.25-3.53 = 1.12 mm
(0.173+0.01-0.139 = 0.044")
Allowable clearace = 0.8-0.9 mm, (0.0315 to 0.0354").

In this case a shims of 0.3 mm (0.012") is removed so that: "S" becomes 1.12-0.3 = 0.82 mm (0.044-0.012 = 0.032").

CYLINDER HEAD

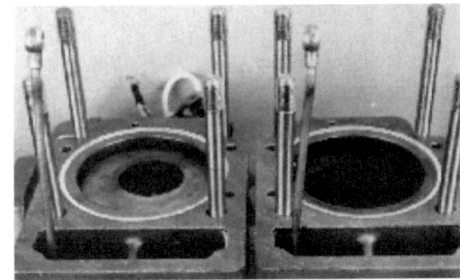

95. Fit new cylinder head gaskets. Make sure that the stud bolts are screwed in properly.

96. Put the cylinder heads on and fit new nuts but do not tighten them.

29

ADJUSTING THE VALVE CLEARANCE

97. Fit the exhaust manifold but only tighten it up enough to align the cylinder heads. **NOTE! Make sure that the gaskets are the right way round.**

Valve clearance with the engine hot:

Inlet 0.30 mm, (0.0118")

Exhaust 0.35 mm, (0.0138")

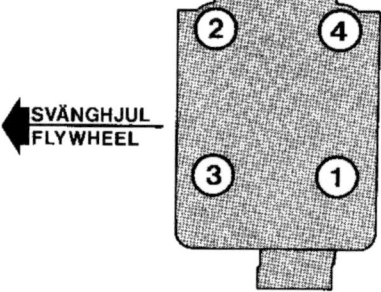

SVÄNGHJUL
FLYWHEEL

100. Turn the engine over in the correct direction of rotation until the valves for one cylinder "rock". Then turn through a further revolution and adjust the valves for this cylinder. Do the same for the other cylinders. After a trial run, the valves should be readjusted whilst the engine is still hot.

98. Tighten the cylinder head nuts in stages of 30, 80 and 110 Nm (3, 8, 11 kpm = 22, 58, 80 lbf.ft.). Tighten the exhaust manifold.

101. Fit the rocker arm covers and check the decompression device as follows:
   A. Remove the oil filler plugs.
   B. Turn the engine over so that the exhaust valve is closed.
   C. Place the handle so that it points upwards.
   D. Loosen the lock nut and screw the adjusting screw upwards. Screw the adjusting screw down again so that it touches the rocker arm. Screw down a further half turn and tighten the lock nut. Replace the oil filler plugs.

NOTE! The decompression device is not adjustable on the D-engines.

99. Check the straightness of the push rods.
Roll the rods on a flat surface. Bent push rods must be replaced.
Fit the push rods and the rocker arm bearing brackets. Connect the oil pipes to the rocker arm shafts.

102. Fit the crankcase breather and the hand starter where applicable.
NOTE! After fitting the hand starter, check that there is backlash between its gearwheel and the drive on the camshaft (in the case of MD17, the check is made through the cover on the hand starter.) If there is no clearance, the number of gaskets under the hand starter is increased until a noticeable clearance is obtained.

FUEL INJECTION PUMP

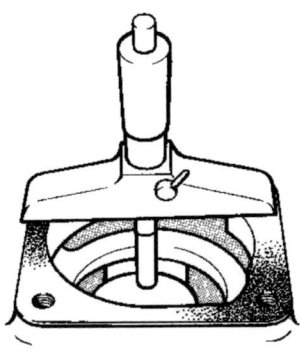

104A. Clean the mating surfaces on the pump and the timing gear cover. Remove the plastic foil from the new gasket and place the gasket on the cover.

B. Measure the distance from the timing gear cover to the base circle of the pump cam (the cam should be turned towards the crankshaft). It is important that the distance should be 82.8±0.2 mm (3.26"±0.008") inclusive of gasket to ensure correct injection angle setting. If the distance is too small increase the number of gaskets. Each gasket is 0.20 mm (0.0079" thick).

If the distance is too great, larger rollers must be fitted to the pump element lifters. These rollers are available in sizes differing by 0.12 mm (0.0047") in diameter. NOTE! If a pump has rollers of different sizes, the diameter of each roller should be increased by the same amount.

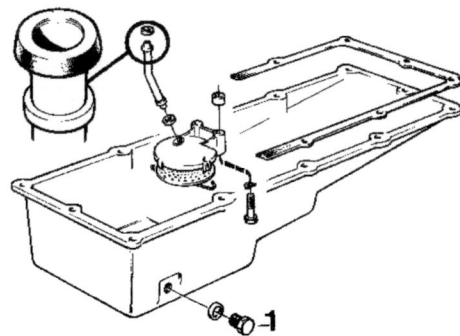

103. MD11: Fit the inspection covers on the crankcase.
MD17: Fit the oil strainer. NOTE! Oil the sealing rings and place them on the ends of the pipe as shown in the illustration. Press the oil pipe into the strainer housing first and then into the crankcase. Fit the oil sump. Tighten the plug "1" (on certain engines).

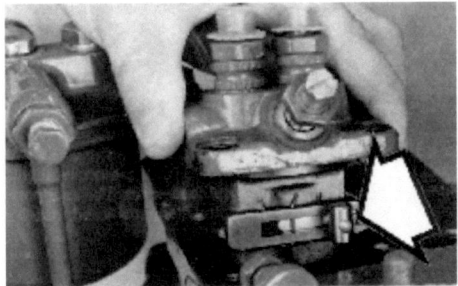

105. Remove the inspection cover on the timing gear cover and fit the injection pump. Make sure that the pin on the control rod is correctly fitted in the governor lever.

CHECKING THE CONTROL ROD TRAVEL

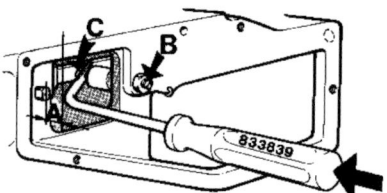

106. A rough adjustment of the injection quantity can be made as follows:
A. Measure the distance (A) from the timing gear cover to the control rod when this is completely pressed in (towards the front of the engine).
B. Repeat the measurement with the control rod in the backward position. NOTE! The cold starting device must not be engaged when taking this measurement. With the MD17, the cold starting device is disengaged by placing the tool 833839 on the pin (C) and pushing forward.
C. The difference between the two dimensions should be:
MD11 7.1±0.1 mm (0.280±0.004")
MD17 6.7±0.1 mm (0.264±0.004")
If there is a dimension stamped on the pump flange, this applies. If necessary adjust by means of the screw (B). Replace the inspection cover.

107. Fit the feed pump and the sea water pump. NOTE! Don't forget to fit the carrier for the sea water pump on MD17. Mount the coolant pipe between the pump and the exhaust manifold.

108. Replace the fuel filter. Fit the injectors, tightening torque: 20 Nm (2 kpm = 14.5 lbf.ft.). Fit all fuel pipes and the lifting eyebolts.
To prevent the injectors seizing it is advisable to spray them with anti-rust agent prior to fitting.

109. MD11: Fit the belt pulley on the flywheel (certain models).
MD11, MD17: Fit the alternator and the V-belt. Connect all electrical cables. MD17: Fit the belt guard (earlier models).

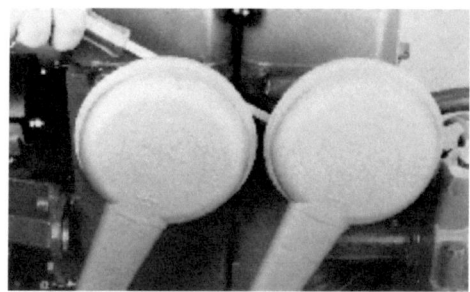

110. Close the cooling water draincocks. Fit the air cleaner.

111. Fill with lubricating oil to the correct level. See "Technical Data" for quantity and grade. NOTE! Do not fill so quickly so as to cause blockage of the ventilation hole (1), (later models).

VENTING THE FUEL SYSTEM

MD11C and MD17C

112. Unscrew the venting screw on the fuel filter by about 4 turns. Watch out for fuel spillage.

115. Unscrew the injector delivery pipe nuts, push the stop control in and set the speed control to full revolutions. Press down the cold start button on MD11. Turn the engine over with the starter motor until fuel comes out of the delivery pipes. Tighten the delivery pipe nuts and start the engine.

MD11D and MD17D

113. Pump fuel out with the hand pump until fuel comes out without air bubbles. Close the vent screw. If the pump does not work well, turn the engine over slightly so as to change the position of the pump driving cam.

116A.
1. Open the vent screw (1 above) on the fine filter. Watch out for fuel spillage. Use pieces of rag (for example) at the point of ventilation.
2. Pump out fuel with the help of the hand pump (2 below) until the fuel comes out without air bubbles. Close the vent screw. If the pump does not work well, turn the engine over slightly so as to change the position of the pump driving cam.

Open the vent screw on the injection pump (3 above) and pump out clean fuel without air. Close the vent screw and open the return pipe screw (pressure equalizing valve) one turn (4 above). Pump out clean fuel without air and close the return pipe screw. Loosen each injector delivery pipe nut and turn the engine over with the starter motor until fuel comes out. Tighten the delivery pipe nut. Start the engine.

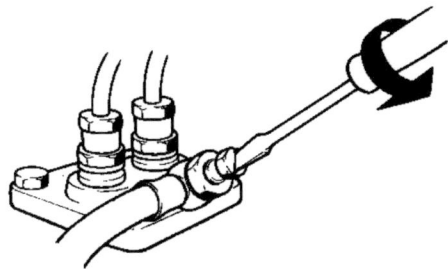

114. Open the vent screw on the injector pump about 2 turns. Pump with hand pump until the fuel comes out without air bubbles. Close the vent screw while pumping.

116B. Feed pump, 2 hand pump.

CHECKING THE INJECTION ANGLE

ADJUSTING ENGINE SPEED

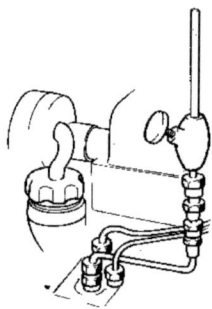

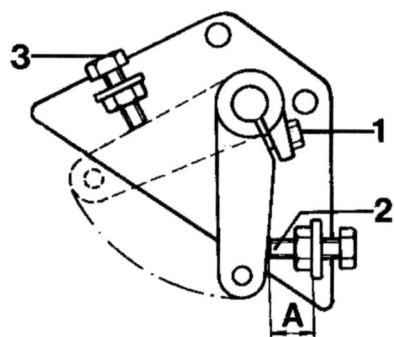

117. Unscrew the rear delivery pipe on the injection pump (nearest the reverse gear) and fit a Wilbär pipe or the level pipe 9993197.

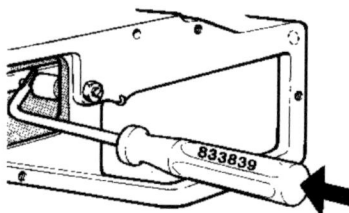

118. MD11: Set the speed control to max. NOTE! The cold start device must not be engaged.
MD17: Remove the inspection cover on the timing gear cover. Push the cold start pin forward using the tool 833839 at the same time as the speed control is set to max.

120A. Allow the engine to warm up and then set the low idling speed adjusting screw (2) so that dimension A in the diagram is 14 mm (0.551").
B. Start the engine and loosen the lock screw (1) on the lever.
C. Turn the lever against the stop (2). Then, using a screwdriver, turn the governor shaft so as to obtain a speed of 12.5-13.5 r/s (750-810 r/min). Tighten the levers' lock screw in this position.
D. Turn the lever up to the adjusting screw (3) and check the high idling speed, which should be MD11C, 17C: 44 r/s (2640 r/min) MD11D, 17D: 46 r/s (2760 r/min) for pleasure use and 42 r/s (2520 r/min) for HD variant. Adjust the speed if necessary.

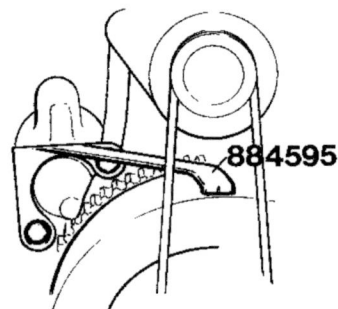

119. Turn the engine over in the direction of rotation until the level pipe is filled with air-free fuel.
Open the level screw on the Wilbär pipe so that the level lies at 25-30 mm (1-1.2") measured upwards. Turn the engine over slowly until the fuel just begins to rise in the pipe. The angle markings on the flywheel should now be at 24-26° B.T.D.C. Adjust the injection angle if necessary by increasing or reducing the number of gaskets under the injection pump.
MD11, use tool 884595. MD17, mark on the belt guard or use tool 884741.

Electrical system

IMPORTANT

The following applies to engines fitted with alternators.

1. Never interrupt the circuit between the alternator and the battery while the engine is running. Otherwise the charging regulator will be ruined. If a main switch is fitted, it must not be switched off until the engine has stopped. Otherwise no cable must be disconnected while the engine is running, since this can also ruin the charging regulator.
2. Check regularly the battery, battery cables and cable terminals. The battery poles should be well cleaned and the terminals tightened and well-greased to ensure continuous function. All cables in general must be well-tightened and dry and sprayed with moisture inhibiting spray. NOTE! On no account must the battery's positive and negative poles be mixed up when the battery is fitted.
3. When starting with the aid of an auxiliary battery, first check to make sure that the auxiliary battery has the same rated voltage as the standard battery. Connect the auxiliary battery to the standard battery with positive to positive and negative to negative. Remove the auxiliary battery when the engine has started. NOTE! On no account must the cables to the standard battery be disconnected in this operation.
4. When carrying out electrical welding on the engine or installation components, the charging regulator cables must first be disconnected and insulated. Both the battery cables must also be disconnected.
5. Before carrying out any repairs on the alternator equipment, always first disconnect both the battery cables. The same applies if the battery has to be rapidly charged.
6. Never test any of the components with a screwdriver or similar tool against a connection to see if there is any spark.

WIRING DIAGRAM

POSITION LIST

1. Temperature gauge
2. Revolution counter
3. Charging warning lamp
4. Oil pressure warning lamp
5. Key switch
6. Switch, instrument lighting
7. Switch, extra equipment
8. Connector
9. Starter motor
10. Alternator
11. Fuse box
12. Main switch
13. Engine speed sender
14. Oil pressure sender
15. Temperature sender
16. Battery

WIRING CODE

Symb.	Colour	mm²	AWG
A	White	6	9
B	Black	1.5	15
B'	Black	0.6	19
C	Red	6	9
C'	Red	35	1
C''	Red	0.6	19
C'''	Red	2.5	13
D	Grey	1.5	15
F	Yellow	1.5	15
G	Brown	1.5	15
H	Blue	4	11
H'	Blue	35	1
H''	Blue	1.5	15
J	Green	1.5	15
J'	Green	0.6	19

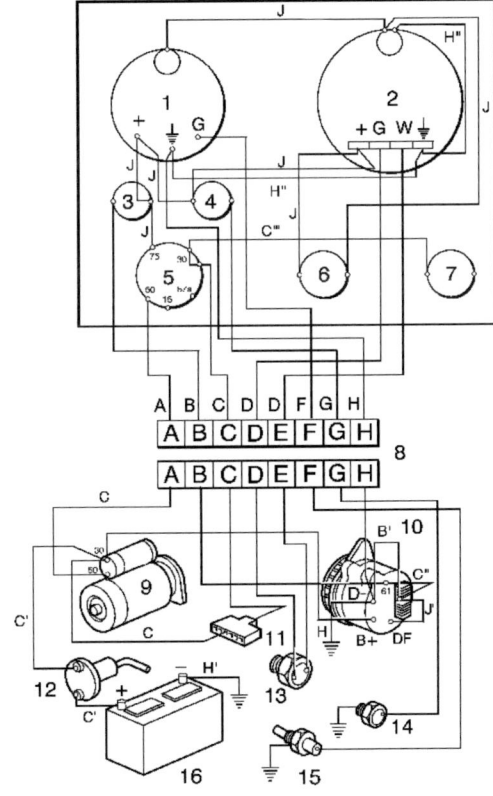

Fault finding table

Engine does not start	Engine stops	Engine does not reach correct working speed on full throttle	Engine runs irregularly or vibrates abnormally	Engine becomes abnormally hot	CAUSE OF TROUBLE
X					Stop control not pressed in. Main switch not closed. Battery discharged. Break in cable or main fuse block.
X	X				Fuel tank empty. Fuel cock closed. Fuel filter blocked.
X	X		X		Water or impurities in fuel. Faulty injectors. Air in fuel system.
		X			Faulty rev. counter. Boat loaded abnormally. Air cleaner blocked. Fouling on boat bottom.
		X	X		Incorrect engine aligning. Propeller damaged.
				X	Obstruction in cooling water intake or cooling jackets. Sea-water pump impeller fault. Thermostat faulty.

Special tools

833839		Tool for disengaging the cold starting device when setting the control rod travel, MD17.
884077		Drift for assembling injector sleeve.
884078		Puller for flywheel, carrier (D-engines) and crankshaft
884081		Injector sleeve extractor
884085		Flaring tool, injector sleeve.
884489		Tool for removing and fitting of main bearings.
884497		Drift for assembling valve sealing rings.
884499		Drift for assembling valve guides.
884560		Drift for removing and fitting rocker arm bearings.
884742		Drift for assembling bearings onto sea water pump shaft, MD17.

884714		Key for oil strainer MD11C.
884581		Fixture for attaching engine to stand, MD17. Use together with engine stand 9992520 and attachment flange 884583.
884604		Fixture for attaching engine to stand, MD11. Use together with engine stand 9992520, attachment flange 884583 and attachment screw 884623.
884579		Tool for dismantling oil filter.
884595 (MD11) 884741 (MD17)		Tool for checking injection pump setting.
884622		Pressing tool for fitting of cylinder liners.
9991459		Drift for removing valve guides.
9992823		Piston assembly ring (standard dimension).
9993197		Level tube for injection pump setting.
9994128		Valve guide reamer.

Technical Data

GENERAL

	MD11C	MD11D	MD17C	MD17D
Type designation				
Output[1] at 41.7 r/s (2500 r/min)	17 kW (23 hp)		26 kW (35 hp)	
at 50 r/s (3000 r/min)		18.4 kW (25 hp)		26.5 kW (36 hp)
Output[2] at 38.3 r/s (2300 r/min) HD-engine	15 kW (20 hp)	15 kW (20 hp)	22 kW (30 hp)	22 kW (30 hp)
MD11D/MSB Output[2] at 41,7 r/s (2500 r/min)		17 kW (23 hp)		
Number of cylinders	2	2	3	3
Bore mm (in)		88.9 mm (3.5")		
Stroke mm (in)		90 mm (3.54")		
Displacement, dm³ (cu.in)	1.12 dm³ (68.35 cu.in)		1.68 dm³ (102.51 cu.in)	
Compression ratio		17.5:1		
Compression pressure at starter motor speed 3.3-4.2 r/s (200-250 r/min)		2-2.5 MPa (20-25 kp/cm² = 284-355 p.s.i.)		
Direction of rotation viewed from flywheel		Clockwise		
High speed idling (overspeed)	2700-2800 r/min	3300-3350 r/min	2700-2800 r/min	3300-3350 r/min
Heavy duty engine	2500-2600 r/min	2800-2900 r/min	2500-2600 r/min	2800-2900 r/min
Low speed idling		750-810 r/min		

CYLINDER LINERS

Material .... Cast iron
Diameter .... 88.90 mm $^{+0.005}_{-0.010}$ mm
3.54 $^{+0.0002"}_{-0.0004"}$

PISTONS

Material .... Aluminium
Diameter, cylinder bore .... 88.78-88.80 mm (3.4953"-3.4961")
Height total mm (in) .... 98 mm (3.858")
Height from centre of gudgeon pin to top of piston mm (in) ... 65 mm (2.559")
Piston clearance in cylinder liner mm (in) .... 0.09-0.13 mm (0.00354-0.00512")

GUDGEON PINS

Diameter mm (in) .... 28.00-28.004 mm (1.10236-1.10252")
Gudgeon pin bearing diameter mm (in) .... 28.014-28.025 mm (1.10291-1.10334")
Clearance gudgeon pin - bearing .... Close running fit

PISTON RINGS

Compression rings, number 3
Oil rings, number 1
The upper compression ring is chrome plated.
Piston ring axial clearance in groove:
1st compression ring .... 0.08-0.11 mm (0.00315-0.00433")
2nd .... 0.06-0.092 mm (0.00236-0.00362")
3rd .... 0.03-0.062 mm (0.00118-0.00244")
Oil ring .... 0.03-0.062 mm (0.00118-0.00244")

Piston ring gap measured in cylinder liner:
1st compression ring .... 0.40-0.55 mm (0.0157-0.0217")
2nd and 3rd .... 0.30-0.45 mm (0.0118-0.0177")
Oil ring .... 0.25-0.40 mm (0.0100-0.0157")

[1] Propeller shaft output, DIN 6270 Leistung B für Dauerbetrieb.
[2] Propeller shaft output for "run-in" engines with reverse gear. DIN 6270 Leistung B für Dauerbetrieb.

	MD11C	MD11D	MD17C	MD17D

CYLINDER HEAD
Material .... Specially alloy cast-iron

CRANKSHAFT AND BEARINGS
Crankshaft axial clearance mm (in) .... 0.08-0.35 mm (0.00315-0.01378")
Main bearings radial clearance mm (in) .... 0.038-0.100 mm (0.00150-0.00394")
Big-end bearings radial clearance mm (in) .... 0.054-0.099 mm (0.00213-0.00390")

MAIN BEARING JOURNALS
Diameter
standard .... 66.646-66.665 mm (2.62386-2.62461")
0.254 mm undersize (0.010") .... 66.392-66.411 mm (2.61386-2.61461")
0.508 mm undersize (0.020") .... 66.138-66.157 mm (2.60386-2.60461 ")
0.762 mm undersize (0.030") .... 65.884-65.903 mm (2.5939-2.5946")

MAIN BEARING SHELLS
Thickness
standard mm (in) .... 2.136-2.145 mm (0.08409-0.08445")
0.254 mm oversize (0.010") .... 2.263-2.272 mm (0.08909-0.08945")
0.508 mm oversize (0.020") .... 2.390-2.399 mm (0.09409-0.094449")
0.762 mm oversize (0.030") .... 2.517-2.526 mm (0.09909-0.09945")

BIG-END BEARING JOURNALS
Diameter
standard mm (in) .... 53.966-53.985 mm (2.12465-2.12539")
0.254 mm undersize (0.010") .... 53.712-53.731 mm (2.11465-2.11539")
0.508 mm undersize (0.020") .... 53.458-53.477 mm (2.10465-2.10539")
0.762 mm undersize (0.030") .... 53.204-53.223 mm (2.09465-2.09539")

BIG-END BEARING SHELLS
Thickness
standard mm (in) .... 1.384-1.391 mm (0.05449-0.05476")
0.254 mm oversize (0.010") .... 1.511-1.518 mm (0.05949-0.05976")
0.508 mm oversize (0.020") .... 1.638-1.645 mm (0.06449-0.06476")
0.762 mm oversize (0.030") .... 1.765-1.772 mm (0.06949-0.06976")

CONNECTING ROD
Axial clearance at crankshaft mm (in) .... 0.05-0.25 mm (0.00197-0.00984")

CAMSHAFT
Axial clearance .... 0.05-0.15 mm (0.00197-0.00591")
Radial clearance in bearing .... 0.03-0.09 mm (0.00118-0.00354")
Bearing journals, diameter
No. 1 .... 31.700-31.725 mm (1.2480-1.2490")
No. 2 .... 46.975-47.000 mm (1.8494-1.8504")
No. 3 .... 48.975-49.000 mm (1.9281-1.9291")
No. 4, (MD17) .... 54.970-55.000 mm (2.1642-2.1654")
The bearings are reamed after pressing in
Cam lift mm (in) .... 5.75-5.85 mm (0.22638-0.23032")

VALVE SYSTEM
Inlet
Valve disc diameter.. 38 mm (1.49606")
Stem diameter mm (in) .... 7.955-7.970 mm (0.31319-0.31378")
Valve seat angle .... 44.5°
Cylinder head seat angle .... 45.0°
Seat width in cylinder head mm (in) .... ca 1.0 mm (0.03937")
Clearance, engine warm mm (in) .... 0.30 mm (0.0118")

	MD11C	MD11D	MD17C	MD17D

Exhaust
Valve disc diameter mm (in) .... 34 mm (1.33858")
Stem diameter mm (in) .... 7.950-7.965 mm (0.31299-0.31358")
Valve seat angle .... 44.5°
Cylinder head seat angle .... 45.0°
Seat width in cylinder head mm (in) .... ca 1.0 mm (0.03937")
Clearance, engine warm mm (in) .... 0.35 mm (0.0138")

DECOMPRESSION DEVICE
Max. downward pressing of exhaust valve
(not adjustable on D-engines) mm (in) .... 0.5 mm (0.01969"

VALVE GUIDES
Length, inlet mm (in) .... 59 mm (2.32283")
exhaust mm (in) .... 52 mm (2.04724")
Bore diameter after assembly and reaming mm (in) ...... 8.0 mm-8.015 mm (0.31496-0.31555")
Height above cylinder head spring surface .... 18 mm (0.70866")
Clearance valve stem-guide
    inlet .... 0.03-0.06 mm (0.00118-0.00236")
    exhaust .... 0.03-0.07 mm (0.00118-0.00276")

VALVE SPRINGS
Free length, unloaded .... 50 mm (1.96850")
loaded with 300±20 N (30±2 kp) (66.139±4.41 lbf). .... 39 mm (1.535432")
560±30 N (56±3 kp) (123.5±6.6 lbf) .... 32 mm (1.25984")

LUBRICATING SYSTEM
Oil capacity, engine inclination 0°
(For inclined engines fill oil to the upper mark on dipstick)
    Engine excl. filter .... 2.6 dm³   4.4 dm³
        (0.7 US galls 0.6 UK galls) (1.16 US galls 0.96 UK galls)
        2.85 dm³   4.65 dm³
    incl. filter .... (0.75 US galls 0.63 UK galls) (1.23 US galls 1.02 UK galls)

Engine incl. RB reverse gear, excl. filter .... 3.0 dm³   4.8 dm³
        (0.79 US galls 0.66 UK galls) (1,27 US galls 1.05 UK galls)
    incl. filter .... 3.25 dm³   5.05 dm³
        (0.86 US galls 0.71 UK galls) (1.33 US galls 1.1 UK galls)

Oil quality acc. to API-system, diesel lubricating oil,
service .... CD (DS)
Viscosity
over +10°C (50°F) Volvo Penta CD oil Double grade ..... SAE 20W/30
under +10°C (50°F) Volvo Penta CD oil Single grade .... SAE 10W
Oil pressure, warm engine idle speed .... 0.1-0.2 MPa (1-2 kp/cm²) (14-28 p.s.i.)
full speed .... 0.2-0.3 MPa (2-3 kp/cm²) (28-43 p.s.i)

LUBRICATION OIL PUMP
Type .... Gear
Spring for reducing valve:
Free length, unloaded .... 40 mm (1.58")
    loaded with 25±2 N (2.5±0.2 kp) (5.5±0.44 lbf) .... 34 mm (1.34")
    35±2 N (3.5±0.2 kp) (7.7±0.44 lbf) .... 31.5 mm (1.24")
Axial gear clearance incl. gasket.................................. 0.03-0.15 mm (0.00118-0.00591")

FUEL SYSTEM
Injection pump manufacturer, Bosch
Injector manufacturer, Bosch hole diameter .... 4 st 0.27 mm (0.01063")
    opening pressure .... MPa $17.0^{+0.8}_{-0}$ $24.6^{+0.8}_{-0}$ $17.0^{+0.8}_{-0}$ $24.5^{+0.8}_{-0}$
    (kp/cm²) (170^{+8}_{-0}) (245^{+8}_{-0}) (170^{+8}_{-0}) (245^{+8}_{-0})
    (p.s.i.) (2418^{+114}_{-0}) (3485^{+114}_{-0}) (2418^{+114}_{-0}) (3485^{+114}_{-0})

Injection angle B.T.D.C .... 24-26°   24.5-26.5°   24-26°   24.5-26.5°
Injection quantity .... 35-36 mm³/stroke at 20°C (68°F) and 16.5 r/s
    (1000 r/min) pump speed
HD-variant .... 33-34 mm³/stroke at 20°C (68°F) and 16.5 r/s
    (1000 r/min) pump speed

FINE FILTER

	MD11C and D	MD17C and D
Type	Spin-on	
Earlier type	Filter insert	

FEED PUMP

Feed pressure at 42 r/s (2520 r/min) .... 65-85 kPa (0.65-0.85 kp/cm^2) (9.25-12.1 p.s.i.)

ELECTRICAL SYSTEM

Battery voltage	12 V	
Battery capacity, pleasure use (starter motor battery) ..	max 70 Ah	max 90 Ah
HD variant (starter motor battery)	max 90 Ah	max 90 Ah
Starter motor output		
pleasure use	1.1 kW (1.47 hp)	1.9 kW (2.55 hp)
HD variant	1.9 kW (2.55 hp)	1.9 kW (2.55 hp)
Alternator		
Output MD11C, MD17C	35 A (490 W)	
MD11D, MD17D,	50 A (700 W)	
Battery electrolyte, specific gravity:		
Fully charged battery	1.275-1.285 g/cm^3 (0.0460-0.0464 lb/in^3)	
Battery to be recharged at	1.230 g/cm^3 (0.0444 lb/in^3)	

COOLING SYSTEM

Thermostat, type	Bellows (Replaceable with wax type)	
WAX from and including engine no	49685	15740
Begins to open at	60°C (140°F)	
Fully open at	74°C (165°F)	
HDHE engine		
Begins to open at	74°C (165°F)	
Fully open at	89°C (192°F)	

WEAR TOLERANCES

Cylinder liners and pistons should be replaced when 0.25 mm (0.010") wear can be measured.

Crankshaft

Permissible out-of-round on main and big-end bearing journals, max	0.06 mm (0.00236")
Permissible taper on main and big-end bearing journals, max	0.05 mm (0.00197")
Max crankshaft end play	0.45 mm (0.01772")

Valves

Valve stem, max permissible wear	0.02 mm (0.00079")
Max. clearance between valve stem and valve guides:	
Inlet valves	0.15 mm (0.00591")
Exhaust valves	0.17 mm (0.00669")
The valve disc edge shall be at least	1.5 mm (0.059")
Distance from valve disc (new valve) to the cylinder head face, max	2.5 mm (0.09843")

Camshaft

Maximum permissible wear in bearing journals and bearings	0.05 mm (0.0020")

TIGHTENING TORQUES

	MD11C and D	MD17C and D
Cylinder head nuts*	110 Nm (11 kpm) (80 lbf.ft.)	
Centre bearing	70 Nm (7.0 kpm) (50 lbf.ft.)	
Big-end bearings	65 Nm (6.5 kpm) (47 lbf.ft.)	
Shield for main bearings	40 Nm (4.0 kpm) (29 lbf.ft.)	
Screw for carrier and carrier drive on crankshaft (for reverse gear)	70 Nm (7.0 kpm) (50 lbf.ft.)	120 Nm (12.0 kpm) C-eng. (87 lbf.ft.) 110 Nm (11.0 kpm) D-eng. (80 lbf.ft.)
Flywheel nut	500 Nm (50 kpm) (369 lbf.ft.)	
Injectors	20 Nm (2.0 kpm) (14.5 lbf.ft.)	
Carrier for water pump	70 Nm (7.0 kpm) (50 lbf.ft.)	320 Nm (32.0 kpm) (231 lbf.ft.)
Cap nuts for valve cover	15 Nm (1.5 kpm) (11 lbf.ft.)	
Nipple for oil filter	40 Nm (4.0 kpm) (29 lbf.ft.)	
Cover for oil strainer MD11 C	70 Nm (7.0 kpm) (50 lbf.ft.)	
MD11 D	120 Nm (12.0 kpm) (87 lbf.ft.)	

* NOTE! Tightening shall be carried out in 3 stages.
1st stage: 30 Nm (3 kpm) (22 lbf.ft.)
2nd stage: 80 Nm (8 kpm) (58 lbf.ft.)
Final stage: 110 Nm (11 kpm) (80 lbf.ft.)

COOLING SYSTEM, DIAGRAMMATIC SKETCH

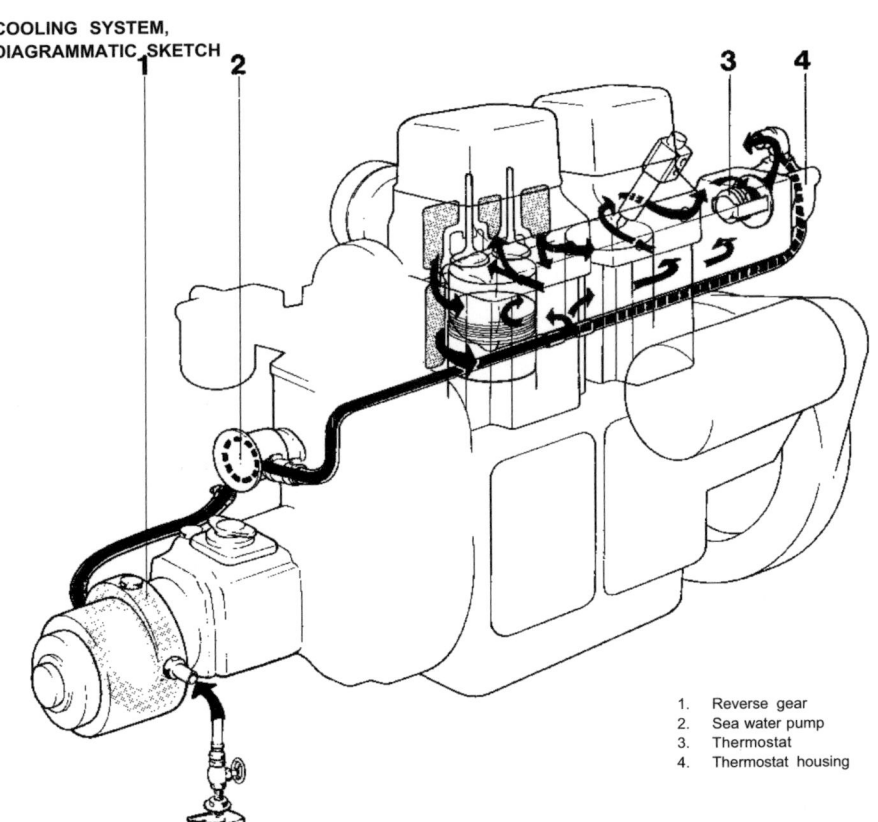

1. Reverse gear
2. Sea water pump
3. Thermostat
4. Thermostat housing